The
From Santa

SONIA BOAL

Illustrations by Jo Hatty

To Luke & Bobby

For the love of Wee Buns

THE LETTER FROM SANTA

First published in Northern Ireland in 2015
by Excalibur Press

This edition published in 2015
by Excalibur Press

Copyright © 2015 Sonia Boal

All rights reserved.

No part of this publication may be reproduced, stored in a retrieval system, or transmitted, in any form or by any means (electronic, mechanical, photocopying, recording or otherwise) without the prior permission of the publisher and copyright holder, nor be otherwise circulated in any form of binding or cover other than that in which it is published.

ISBN-13: 978-0-9935015-3-1
ISBN-10: 0993501532

Formatting & layout by
by Excalibur Press

Excalibur Press
Belfast, Northern Ireland

excaliburbelfast@gmail.com
07982628911 | @ExcaliburPress
www.excaliburpress.co.uk

THE LETTER FROM SANTA

Santa was in his workshop, doing a clear-out. There was a load of old junk lying around from last Christmas, and he needed to make way for all the new toys his elves were due to start making for this year.

He had just moved a big box of wood out of the way when he heard a big, loud, plop!

THE LETTER FROM SANTA

A puddle the size of a Christmas cake had formed on the workshop floor and as Santa stood there looking at it; another drip fell from the ceiling and landed right on his nose.

"What on Earth is this?" exclaimed Santa, wiping his nose, "I need to find out where this water is coming from"

Santa rang his bell and an Elf came running into the workshop.

"Jingles, have you seen this leak, you're the Elf and Safety Rep, do you know what's causing it?"

The bells at the end of Jingles hat jangled as he shook his head no.

"Right" said Santa, "There's nothing else for it; we need to go up onto the roof, dig down through the snow, find the hole, and fix it."

Jingles looked at Santa with big wide eyes.

"We are at the North Pole, there must be 10 metres of snow up there!" he said.

"Better bring a big spade then" said Santa, who was pulling on his boots, "Come on, that puddle is only getting worse".

When they went outside Santa and Jingles got an enormous shock.

Instead of finding lots of snow, they found themselves on an island surrounded by water!

"What on Earth?" shouted Santa and Jingles together.

"At the North Pole, there should be ice and snow as far as we can see, what is going on?

"Go and see if the reindeer are ok, I'm going to try and find out why this ice is melting".

As Santa was at his desk reading his news reports, Jingles came back into the workshop.

THE LETTER FROM SANTA

"Do you want the good news or the bad news Santa"? Santa looked at him over the rim of his spectacles, "you choose" he said.

"Well, the good news is that the reindeer are fine and I've patched up the hole in the roof. But the bad news is that we have a problem getting all the materials we need to make the new toys for

Christmas. I can't find anywhere that can send us the supplies we need before January".

Santa sat back into his chair and sighed. "I was afraid of that" he said.

"I think it is linked to the ice melting. The people of the world have used up so many of the world's resources, that there is hardly anything left, and when they finish with their stuff they just throw it away.

"The rubbish ends up in a landfill site which gives off gas.

"It in turn is heating the planet up and making the ice caps melt. It's a terrible problem.

"There are tropical islands that will go underwater as the sea level rises, and there is a great big garbage patch full of plastic in the middle of the Pacific Ocean, the animals that live there are dying as they have to swim through a plastic soup. I don't know where to start with this, the problem is bigger than one person can solve.

Mrs Claus came in as Jingles and Santa were talking things over. "Are you checking your list dear? It's already starting to grow".

Santa looked glum, "I think we are going to have to cancel Christmas this year sweetheart, we need snow for the reindeer and the sleigh to work, and even worse, we don't have anything to make new toys with. It doesn't look like Christmas is going to be much fun at all."

Mrs Claus scratched her head and looked straight at Santa. "You have to make this work" she said, you are Father Christmas, and all the Children in the world are counting on you, just the same as they do every year. What about using some of the materials left over from last year?

Santa had a look at one of the boxes he had moved out of the workshop. "Hmmm" he thought to himself, "if I just cut that wood up a bit, and there's a bit of wiring left over, which I could use, and I wonder if that bit of plastic could be bent; oh good, yes!"

In no time at all Santa had made a remote control boat out of an old plastic bottle, a coat hanger, and a scrap of material. With a little bit of Christmas magic, it looked sleek, and fast and perfect for racing on a boating lake. Mrs Claus nodded her approval. "Good, I know just the child who will love that" she said, that's a brilliant start, but you will need a bit more if you are going to get to the bottom of your list.

Jingles jumped up "I have an idea Santa", he shouted "we have a big container of wrong toys from the past few years; they didn't work right so we didn't send them out, and maybe we could use those to make new toys?"

"Perfect" said Santa, "let's get started on this now". Santa and Jingles worked all day without stopping and by early evening they had a pile of toys that would fill a room, ready to be wrapped up ready for Christmas Day.

As they stood back and looked at their work Santa began to look sad again. "What's wrong?" asked Jingles, "I thought you would be really happy with all these new toys, this has been some of your best ever work!"

"I am proud of it" said Santa, "but the thing is, it still isn't enough. We have used up all of our leftovers, and we have recycled all of our old toys, but it's not enough for every child to receive a gift on Christmas Day. We need more broken toys!"

Jingles looked forlorn. "Where are we going to get more broken toys from?" he said. "What we really need is for every child to send us one broken toy, and that way we would have enough for everybody, and maybe even a little to spare.

THE LETTER FROM SANTA

"Brilliant Jingles!" yelled Santa, "Just brilliant! That is exactly what we will do. We will get every child to take an old broken toy to their local recycling centre; we can collect these, and recycle them into brand new toys."

So, very carefully Santa wrote a letter to all of the children on his list.

Then he thought about the children who were on his list years ago and were now parents and sent it to them too.

Every letter was individual, but most of them went a bit like this;

Dear _____

I hope you are well, and looking forward to Christmas. Thank you so much for the mince pie and shortbread last year, it was very thoughtful. Rudolph and the other reindeer really appreciated the carrot and we are all looking forward to visiting you again this Christmas Eve.

Here at the North Pole we have noticed that there is a lot less snow than usual, and a lot more water. It's a big problem; the Polar Bears are very grumpy and need their ice back. On the other side of the World, some of the islands of the Pacific are about to go underwater as the glaciers that are melting here are making the sea level rise there.

In the middle of the Pacific Ocean there is an enormous area that is like a dirty plastic soup which is killing the birds, fish and animals that live there. But most worrying is the fact that it is really difficult to get the things we need to make toys for this Christmas. We really need your help.

We think that if every child takes an old broken toy to their local recycling centre rather than putting it in the bin we can begin to change things.

If every grown up recycled more of their rubbish and all of their food waste we could make a really big change.

And if everybody only bought what they really needed, turned off lights when they go out of a room and walked occasionally rather than using the car, we could have a healthier world and fitter bodies to enjoy it.

I really hope that you can find something and take it to your recycling centre, as we can only fix this if everybody does their bit; and there's a better chance that you'll be on my "good list" if you do.

Take care of yourself
Lots of love
Santa

Once the letters were posted, there was nothing to be done except wait. Santa, Jingles and Mrs Claus tried to keep themselves busy as best they could, but they were nervous.

Then, the phone started ringing. Recycling centres all over the world were beginning to fill up with toys.

Children everywhere were looking for broken toys and other waste but instead of putting it in the bin and sending it to landfill, they were recycling it. Santa was overjoyed.

"Hooray!" he shouted, "There is hope after all!" and with that he, Jingles and the other elves raced off to the workshop to start work on the new toys.

Mrs Claus smiled to herself as she watched them disappear with a load of toys.
Then she shivered and had to rub a bit of heat back into her arms.

As she wrapped her cardigan a bit tighter round herself she thought "I'm cold! I haven't been cold for weeks" and she raced to the window to look out at the weather. Sure enough, the first snowflakes were beginning to flutter down and the sea was beginning to freeze over again.

"It's working Santa" she shouted on the way down to the workshop.

THE LETTER FROM SANTA

"It's really working! The parents and other grown-ups must finally be recycling their rubbish, driving less and not wasting energy. It's amazing how quickly it's beginning to have an effect. I'm so pleased!

Santa went to the window and smiled. He was glad to see things improving but he knew that this was just a start, people would have to keep recycling and saving energy all the time and not just once if they wanted to protect the world's vulnerable people and places.

He thought about the Great Pacific Garbage Patch, and about a little boy who had asked him for some Meccano and a paddling pool some years ago. "He grew up to be a marine engineer" thought Santa, I should check in on him and see if he has any ideas about how we fix this problem".

He looked at his watch. "Is that the time?" he exclaimed "We need to get a move on with these toys".

And with that, Santa, Jingles, and Mrs Claus joined the other elves in the workshop, sorting the old toys, making an ideas list of things they could be tuned into, and transforming the rubbish into wonderful brand new toys.

THE LETTER FROM SANTA

That year, the boys and girls on Santa's good list had their best ever Christmas.

The toys were better, more interesting and much more fun than ever before, and everyone was happy.

Santa watched from his house at the North pole and smiled.

He thought about some of the other problems in the world like trees being cut in the rain forests, and animals like Orang-utans and tigers losing their homes.

That can go into next year's letter he thought sleepily, and with that he closed his eyes for a moment and took a well earned rest.

About The Author

Sonia Boal graduated from Coventry University with a BSc in Environmental Science in 1992.

She returned to her native Northern Ireland, and volunteered for a number of environmental organisations before taking a job with NI2000, an environmental NGO, as their Education Officer.

Here Sonia was responsible for a range of projects including organising NI's first Green Christmas fair which allowed visitors to buy everything from the Christmas tree to the turkey from local sustainable suppliers.

She currently works for Belfast City Council as a recycling officer, where amongst other things, she commissioned local artist Terry Bradley to create a designer reusable shopping bag for Belfast.

THE LETTER FROM SANTA

Her life changed beyond recognition in 2008 with the birth of her first son. Now, as a mother of two and a Stepmum of two more, Sonia looks for ways to teach her own children about what is important, and how they fit into the world we live in.

Stories, more than anything else capture the imagination; so she wrote a story for her boys to help them understand some of the issues that they will have to deal with as they grow up.

When telling the story to her own boys, Sonia noticed that they became most engaged if the letter was "addressed" to them, that's why it's been left blank, so that you can do the same.

Of course it also led to a few extra trips to the local recycling centre that she hadn't planned, but that's no bad thing.